Reflections Of

THOMAS ALLEN FRITH

authorHOUSE®

AuthorHouse™ LLC
1663 Liberty Drive
Bloomington, IN 47403
www.authorhouse.com
Phone: 1-800-839-8640

Published by AuthorHouse   01/24/2014

ISBN: 978-1-4918-5587-4 (hc)
ISBN: 978-1-4918-5598-0 (sc)
ISBN: 978-1-4918-5599-7 (e)

Library of Congress Control Number: 2014901481

Dedicated To

This book is dedicated to my beautiful and loving wife, Beverly, for your support, understanding, and encouragement. You have been by my side in all of my efforts. It is a privilege to share my love and life with you as we continue to travel, live and work together on future endeavors. Without you, I would not be the person that I am today.

All my love to you, BB.

PREFACE

Having been born to a family living in the country, I grew up enjoying nature and animals. I spent many hours walking across pastures and thru woods searching for wildlife and observing the unique events of nature that were there to explore. From sunrise to the evening hours, there was never a time that I would not stop to watch an animal or observe something in the sky.

As I grew older, I became fascinated with various machinery and how they worked. I became attached to current events related to the space technology. I took those concepts and ideas and built structures or role played as my interest spread to the fast pace of technology. My interest led me to write about my thoughts in the form of poetry.

The invasion of the new rock music of The Beatles and the English rock bands again sparked my interest in putting thoughts to pen. I begin writing music hoping for the big break into a music career. There were numerous songs written which somewhere along the way were lost or destroyed. However, my poetry writing continued.

I took time away from my writing to begin a life in the military and education. It wasn't until I decided to retire from the public sector that I began to write again. I wrote several love poems for my wife. This lead me to begin writing in prose, as well as screenplays.

I searched my past files for poems I had written earlier in life and began to add a few more. When my collection began to accumulate, I shared many of my poems with others. The feedback was positive. It was then I decided I would publish a few select poems and took the step to create this book.

I chose a selection of rhyming poems, that covers a vast area of interest. I chose not to include my love poems I had written to my wife. They are our personal poems which have special meanings to us.

Even though I continue to write poetry, I also do writings in other areas such as comedy, drama, suspense, as well as non-friction. Writing is now a true career for me as I move from the sunrise to the evening of my life.

This collection of poems from the past, as well as, the current are here for all to enjoy. Some may stretch you mind while others will tease you to explore your inner person and make you look at things a little differently.

Enjoy.

TABLE OF CONTENTS

NATURE

CLOUDS

The clouds move so freely about,
If to run and give a shout.
The wind thus blow them across the sky,
I watch and wave goodbye.

We do not know where they go
All we know is they are pushed as the wind thus blow.
They seem to grow high into the air,
Provides design and moves with flare.

One is white and one blue
Each tells you what they can do.
Some are friendly and tame at best.
They will give you fun and rest.

Some are bad and a scary sight,
Makes one go to bed with some fright.
Clouds can help the farmer so,
Make fruit and vegetables grow.

Clouds can produce damaging wind,
Hail and snow it can send.
Clouds may be beautiful to the sight,
Mixed with one flying a kite.

As the cloud grows and matures,
I do not know its intention for sure.
I watch as it passes by,
I lay and watch them in the sky.

FALL

Bright orange, yellow and colorful leaves,
Nature pulls fall out of its sleeve.
Beautiful valleys and silent hollers,
Span out in radiant color.
Mountains covered in sights of fall,
We try to take it in all in all.
A color scene hard to find,
Only in fall or left behind.
The October wind blow silently by,
The limbs and leaves and into the sky.
Leaves of red mixed within,
Only to turn and see them again.
Orange and yellow spread about,
I look below and begin to shout.
Oh wow! What a great scene,
Far sights that I once deemed.
I sit and observe the colors before me,
A carpet of color spread out for me to see.
Red, Yellow, orange and brown,
Spread out over the valley I found.
I take a mental picture in my mind,
Knowing again a scene never to find.
The cool air covers the vast valley below,
With colors of beauty in my mind, I know.
How the beauty can be describe,
I cannot say even with a bribe.
Beauty oh Beauty is the color display,
Various colors I describe if I may.

Red as a fire truck down the road is gone,
Yellow as the sun as the day moves on.
Brown adds to the artist color of array,
Green mixed in to this I see today.
Orange spreads out across the dale,
All mixed with a sight that leaves other things pale.
Rise up and walk away from the view,
Of the range of color and variety of hue.
I wish I could spend more time to see,
A view so beautiful that encourages me.
To take my time as I walk away,
Hoping to return and view another day.

WINTER'S PATH

On a cold winter morning I walk the road,
At the point of freezing I am told.
The white ground glistening it in the sun,
Maybe catch snowballs and have some fun.
There is not a single footprint pressed therein,
Just a nice shine and a small cold breeze of wind.

I take a step on the fresh white snow,
And on to my destination I do go.
As I look to the right, a rabbit I do see,
As it spies me and off it tries to flee.
I see him hop and jump in the air,
To get across the deep snow so fair.

Away he hops to get on his way,
Behind a tree and then a bale of hay.
I travel on down the road,
Feeling the depths of the chilling cold.
The trees limbs bend to the weight,
Of the snow on it, as it adds more flakes.

The weather is getting worse as I head along,
Trying to get away and back to home.
I struggle in the deep snow with each step,
I begin to think I need more help.
I am about to feel I had failed,
I hear a great yell as it welded.

My wife was wondering if I would make it,
She knew that I was able and fully fit.
Of course as the cold weather closed in,
She was wondering if I would win.
I see the light between the blowing flakes,
I struggle more with all it takes.

I am met with a warm hug that night,
I make the last step up each flight.
The stairs were frozen from the brisk cold,
The wind, the snow and all so bold.
Home I am, to be there at last,
I sit and warm and reflect on the past.

MISTY LAKE

The misty fog upon the lake,
I look and memory sight I do take.
The light haze of drifting mist,
I shade my eyes with a half fist.
I scan the waters for signs of a trail,
Everything is misty and very pale.
I look for a way to get to the other side,
That path in the mist continues to hide.
I take a step adjusting my sight,
Not knowing if that decision is wrong or right.
I glare into the distant as far as I can,
Only with my eyesight as I do scan.
I see a few trees peeking out of the haze,
A pond of water creating a maze.
I step again to get a better sight,
Wonder if I should worry or begin to fight.
To myself I ask if I am lost,
I must continue at all cost.
I cannot give up on my flight,
Do I go straight or do I go right?
In far the distance, I see something like a stick,
What is that? I wonder as I stare at it.
It begins to glow across the lake,
Ah! A path. Do I try to make?
It gets clearer as I take each step,
Is this what I hope, something to help?
I finally can see the object clear,
A sight I want and love so dear.
The object is clear inside the mist,
Oh, it is my car I did miss.

AROMA

Oh the sweet aroma I do smell,
An odor I recall very well.
Such a smell my mind spend on,
To memories that all are gone.
Maybe once or twice I can say,
That the smell is one if I may.
It's a preference over any others,
As my heart begins to flutter.
The memory of the smell I recall,
Is not the memory, I think, or at all.
You see the smell is one of favor,
And one I like and begin to savor.
It makes my mind begin to wonder,
As to the smell I do ponder.
Is it a smell of a beautiful spring flower?
Is it made from the grainy flour?
Maybe a smell for the garden outdoors,
Maybe one from cleaning the floors.
Can it be my wife's sweet perfume?
I wonder and can only assume.
Whatever it is that smells so sweet
It's a smell that cannot be beat.

Thomas Allen Frith

LONELY TREE

The tree stands in the field all alone,
Trimmed and shaped in a fullness tone.
Standing so tall although it is actually small,
There to be seen by each and all.

A tree so green upon the snow,
Nice and pretty as it grows.
A tree that anyone would be proud,
Resting among the touching clouds.

The daylight shine from afar,
A shade is created but this par.
But this shade is special you see,
It shades you and me.

The tree stands so proud and tall,
To be enjoyed by one and all.
There are those who do not care,
They want the scenery to be empty and bare.

A bird has made it a home with a nest,
Maybe a robin with its red glowing breast;
Maybe a bluebird with feathers so blue;
Maybe just any bird, for that is true.

The tree stands there all alone,
It will be missed once it is gone.
The next generation doesn't see the same,
Trees are in the way and are to blame.

Progress is interfered by them all,
Down they come and hard they fall.
Not just one or two they say,
Wait till they are all gone someday.

A tree is needed, one does not see,
It is too late, if we don't let them be.
There is this one lone tree,
Looking lonely and a sight to see.

MISTY SIGHT

Across the valley in the misty day's air,
I see ghostly figures way over there.
Towering high are gray figures into the sky,
The images expands to be way up high.
Misty by fog and as quiet as can be,
The misty images spread out as far as I can see.

Behind the dam of the lake down the hill,
There flies a large bird with a big bill.
The air is thick, very moist and wet,
I walk out, wet I would get.
The scenery is of a perfect winter day,
But the snow is missing and held at bay.

If the ground was to covered with snow,
My image of winter will definitely grow.
Going back to the image I see,
Is it a grove of big oak trees?
Standing tall in the misty rainy sky,
A lone bird flies lazily by.

The scene is one as I sit and look out,
Sit warmly on my porch, which is no doubt.
I see through the pane window glass,
I see another bird fly past.
The misty scenery spreads out wide as far,
I spy. I ask, Is that a star?

Shining between the mist as the day light fades,
Into night as if it was made.
Stationary shining in the misty sight,
Shining its best and all its might.
Time passes without knowledge or care,
I sit on my porch just being there.

The ghostly figure still sitting there,
I watch through the misty air.
I do not want to leave such a winter sight,
I must; I do; get up and take my flight.
The images I see are just big oak trees,
And I leave them and inside I will be.

Thomas Allen Frith

NOVEMBER RAIN

I sit in my swing upon my porch,
Wondering what relief from the summer scorch.
November rain pouring upon the ground,
To seek a place it may have found.

I watch the rain come gently down,
Although to catch upon my face a frown.
November Rain is actually rare,
Trying to get accepted as being fair.

I sit and watch the large rain drops,
Upon the sidewalk the drops goes flop.
November rain welcome so much,
Wishing it would help flowers and such.

An inch at first and then there was two,
I sit and then put on my shoes.
November rain may come a little late,
I cannot change its fate.

It seems as no end to be,
At least as far as I can see.
November rain is what it is about,
I begin to wonder and have my doubts.

I decide to go inside and let it rain,
Because it is now becoming a pain.
November rain is far too much,
As it hits my feet with its touch.

The cold and wet droplets hit my feet,
Only spring rain could it beat.
November rain is what it is about,
As I go in and enough I shout.

MORNING AIR

The morning was crisp and a little wet,
Not a day that one had met.
In the early dawn the sun shines dim,
I see it peeking on the rim.

The rain did come and now is gone,
Was it a shower or was I wrong?
The deck is wet with small puddles,
The chilly wind makes one want to cuddle.

It may be cold by what they say,
It will get colder during the day.
Will the rain turn to snow?
Let the geese be on the go.

To the south as they fly,
I see them rise into the sky.
It is a sign the winter is near,
This is weather for me and my dear.

She and I enjoy the cold,
It is another story to be told.
I go back inside to hide from the chill,
To gain my thoughts and my will.

I think about the day that may be,
I'm not sure if I do want to see.
I wonder in my head,
I decided to go back to bed.

RAINBOW

Rain comes and rain goes,
I dress for the rain in my rain clothes.
When the rain has gone away,
It will be back another day.

As I look into the sky,
What is it that I spy?
Red, Blue and colors of gold,
Into an arc, it is mold.

I cannot say why it looks so good,
As I uncover my head from its hood.
I stop from my daily pace,
The image is shown upon my face.

I sit and stare at the sight,
Wishing that maybe I could take flight.
To travel upon the arc of red,
And to end at the pot in flower beds.

There it is so high in the sky,
A rainbow is what I spy.
Its colors so bright and bold,
But no flood will be I am told.

From side to side the colors show,
Into the sky in an arc it goes.
I now sit and watch the display,
As lightning flashes on this rainy day.

The dark blue clouds in the back,
A sound of thunder provides a crack.
All this in the background behind,
Where else would that be found?

A rainbow comes about,
Displays it color and gladly shout.
The rain is gone for now it seems,
As the sun shines upon it beams.

RAIN

Listening to the sound on the roof,
Is it someone or Santa's reindeer hoofs?
It cannot be them because it is not time,
But to my window I try to find.

The noise I heard, I heard before,
Wondering what, I wish could I hear more.
Cause out my window I did see,
Rain pouring out of the sky with glee.

It is raining dogs and cats,
Inside safe and dry is where I am at.
A person out in this wet mason,
Will be soaked faster than soon.

As I watch the rain pour down,
I actually do not have a frown.
It was been weeks since it has rained,
The dryness has become a major pain.

I see the earth soak up the raindrops,
Did I see a fish fall and flop?
No I didn't see one do so,
But I did see the water go.

Down the hill and out the ditch,
If I could hold it and make a switch.
I would divert the flow of the land,
I need it to flow away from the sand.

Down the canal in my backyard,
But it is almost impossible and hard.
The dear Lord had already design,
The flow I wish but only find.

It flows to the left not to the right,
Even when I try with all my might.
I just have to accept this event with defeat,
And not to try to fuss and repeat.

Changing a natural wish of God,
Just look in the sky and give a reverent nod.
I accept the rain, the amount, and when,
As it starts to pour again.

There is the sound back on the roof,
It is only hard rain and no hoofs.
I turn and accept the friendly noise
As I stop and listen in my poise.

SEASON

The snow piles up upon the grass,
And the sound of smoothing brass.
The moon beams shine upon the white,
How do we know is it true or right?

The pine tree is cut and ready,
For decorating by one's daddy.
Gold and red and yellow too,
Is placed as he does his due.

The light are hung in their place,
As shopper buy at a fast pace.
Trying to beat the deadline of that night,
And trying to not argue and fight.

Peace on Earth and memories are told,
Maybe not if I am so bold.
We wish it was true this night,
As we glance upon that special sight.

Do we remember what the meaning is?
As we go about our daily biz.
The meaning has lost its glory might,
As we celebrate this special night.

It may not have its meaning of the past,
We hope that this one is not the last.
As we gather with our loves ones,
To cheer and cry and have some fun.

Goodbye to a year that has left,
Hoping we do not think of just ourselves.
So long to all as we go our way,
Merry Christmas is all I can say.

SETTING SUN

The sun shining in through the window,
Listening to the strong wind blow.
The shadow from the oak tree,
Cast a moving shadow on me.
Seems to move too slow.

The sun falling in the western sky,
I watch it set as if to spy.
The bright orange glow hanging low at sight,
It seems to fight with all its might.
Try to hide and unleash the tie.

The sun disappearing behind the trees,
Causing the night it just has to be.
Light will dim and change to black,
Sometime later it will be back.
To the east I will wait and see.

Thomas Allen Frith

THE TREE

I sit looking at your leaves,
I sit and cry and even grieve.
You look so beautiful in your green spring wear,
Do you know that I really do care?
Standing so tall and covered in grace,
You go about your normal pace.
Your limbs swing in the gentle breeze,
Even if the air makes me sneeze.
I watch you in your magnificent beauty,
If it is my full and only duty.
The swag of your trunk and leafy hands,
Your leaves move like blowing sand.
I do grieve as I think about tomorrow,
Until I know, I will sit in silent sorrow.
For I know your beauty will not last,
As your leaves will leave and create a past.
You lose your cover so green,
For sure, it has been seen.
Even as I do see this very day,
I have one more thing to say.
I know your leaves are gone for now,
They will return, I know not how.

THE MOON

Look over yonder upon the horizon.
There is a big moon and it is arising.
Look how large and yellow it shines,
Like a big treasure that is hard to fine.

Over the hill and the trees it peeks,
Acting like it is playing hide and seek.
It casts its shadows from behind the trees
It touches feelings inside me.

Why does the moon look this way?
I have my thoughts but one might say,
It is God's gift for you and me.
He watches over us and wants us to see.

His great creation in the sky,
Is a way to watch us as the night flies by.
This may be his way,
To tell us what he has to say.

He uses the moon to give us light,
To reminds us of his love all in spite.
Of all the things we do against him,
Our selfishness and our whims.

He places it there to remind us through
Of the place reserved for us in gold.
The bright sight of the moon
Is to remind us he is coming for us soon.

SKY

You sit there so bright and blue,
I don't know what you do.
Some days and nights you are so bad,
That internally makes me sad.
Other days you are so pleasing,
The day goes by without any sneezing.
Your patterns varies as does the nights,
At a distance you shine your heavenly lights.
It makes me feel so calm and serene,
As I glaze upon your nightly scene.
Who could have made this sight so true?
Other than God that prepared it for you.
There are times we avoid your sights,
When you gives us that night fright.
Its sounds, rumble, and bright light flash,
I hide my head and inside I dash.
After you had your fiery fit,
I watch and in your mist I sit.
After such a disorderly scene,
You make yourself so nice and serene.
Your mornings bring a nice blight sight,
The sun comes up and provide the light.
The evening as the sun goes down,
We are amazed by the sights with no sound.
You seem not to tire with what you do,
Who are you? Yes, Who?

THE STORM

The storm gives her warning of what is to be.
The looks and sounds scares a little in me.
The high black clouds towering in the sky above,
Sends the birds away including the dove.
Bright lightning flash dancing across the sky,
Only to disappear as if to hide.
Here comes the roar and thunder moan,
The flash gave pain and made it groan.
The frequency of the flash and moaning sound,
Get closer and louder as rain hits the ground.
The wind begins to send it mighty strength,
To discard everything through its length.
The rain pours down like a waterfall,
Flooding the ground, my hair, and all.
Once the storm passes so gallantly by,
The air smells fresh and there is a clear sky.
The storm that once gave me a fright,
Has disappeared into a new fresh night.

WIND

The wind gently blows on me,
I look around but there is nothing to see.
Who was it that got my attention this time?
I search and search but only to find.
No one was near or even nearby,
I eagerly try to find someone to spy.
Another gentle breeze begins to blow,
That was when I had my answer I know.
It was no one that give me a touch.
It was nature's way to say I like you much.

LEAVES

Leaves are falling down to the ground,
The tree seems to give off a frown.
The season of green is gone once more,
I watch out my front door.

Leaves lay one on top of one,
All falls down when fall is done.
Now the problem of what to do,
I ponder and wonder if I knew.

All these leaves lying there for me,
Determines if I rake or what is to be.
Let the wind blow them around,
They still are on the ground.

I rake them in a pile,
This will take me awhile.
If I do then there's options for me,
Maybe burn or compost, I will have to see.

If I leave them on the ground there,
The wind could blow them in the air.
If the wind is strong enough,
They could be resistant and tough.

I watch the leaves there on the ground,
Wondering if a rake could be found.
I ponder that I would decide one day,
Not at this time as I go on my way.

Country

THE BRIDGE

There stands an old iron rusty bridge,
Up and over that next high ridge.
The rusty rails towering way up high,
As if to reach for the morning sky.

Its body is made of rotten wood,
Would not let one pass if they could.
Broken planks lay across the dusty trail,
Rusty iron upon each of the rails.

It stands so boldly majestic but alone,
The days of luster and glory all gone.
Have they actually gone away?
Maybe they will return another day.

Someone has decided to take care of you,
At least one, two or maybe a few.
You still have the strength that it takes,
Not to let one fall through, crash or break.

You see someone does really care,
To shine those rails that lift in the air.
Replace the planks with all new ones,
You will smile when they are done.

A little paint and a little repair,
Lifts your spirit and your despair.
You get a new look and full flair,
As one sees you shine over there.

CHURCH BY THE ROAD

There stands a church so lonely and still.
All the people gone. Is it God's will?
The doors are shut and not a sound,
Not a person or a human around.
If you stop and go inside,
There is nothing there that will hide,
A past of people that worshiped there.
Where have they gone, yes where?

The community that once was around,
Is now nothing but bare ground.
With all the families moving out,
How could the church give out a shout?
"Do not leave me here alone,
I need someone to call me home."
The people don't hear the desperate concern,
With their future, they go, with their yearn.

There stands an old building by the road,
With many a story to be told.
A child was raise and spent much time,
That child is now hard to find.
What is left is an empty pew,
Evidence of a mission and dues,
Of people gone from the past,
And a future outside its grasp.

I leave the church beside the road
I look back as I am told
This will be my last time here,
I need to keep this moment dear.
I walk away to my car,
Knowing I am leaving and going far.
Not to return to this very place,
I return to the human rat race.

Thomas Allen Frith

SAD COUNTRY ROADS

I travel many a road in my life,
Along my side has been my wife.
I love to see the scenery there,
Feel and enjoy the fresh night air.
They are forgotten or so I am told,
All alone, sad country roads.

The winding curves and holes in the ground,
Not a smooth path can be found.
Trees grow along the way,
There are round bales of hay.
The sight is there or so I am told,
All alone, sad country roads.

Where they go is left to be found,
As they cover many a ground.
They seem to go forever on their way,
To a home up the hill far away.
If this is true as I am told,
All alone, sad country roads.

You take one down its lonely path,
The toll that it takes, you call it only wrath.
It divides from one and into three,
Oh where they go and where they be.
All I know is what I am told,
All alone sad country roads.

The three turn into more as they go,
With some ending before I get cold.
Some wanders and have no end in sight
I try to travel to the end, if I might.
All I know is what I am told,
All alone sad country roads.

DOWN THE ROAD

Down the Road that goes forever,
The end seems to come; never.
I travel the winding narrow lane,
While I wonder if I am sane.
To travel such an abandoned trail,
Wondering if my eyesight has failed.
I strain my eye to see what is ahead of me,
All I see are low hanging limbs of tree.
As they start caving in,
I ponder where I have been.
The road ditch seem to disappear,
I wonder and begin to fear.
On each side of this road
Limbs reach in, all so bold.
There is almost no lane at all,
It narrows down to be so small.
I ease my way slowly ahead,
I begin to wonder if this road is dead.
I stop my car upon the sight,
I wonder if a turnaround is a might.
I do not think I can continue on,
Because the road is now all gone.
Right before me is a fence.
With trees lining it very dense.
I have gone as far as it be,
There is no road to see.
There is only one way out of here,
If I just stop and disappear.
To retrace my path and my fate
To return home before it is late.

LONELY ROAD

As I drive down this lonely road in the early morn,
There isn't a person, a car, not even a horn.
Since leaving the busy city life,
The world is easy and lack of strife.
A light I spy far in the distance,
It is gone in just one instance.
I glance to the heavenly skies,
I wonder who is up there as a spy.
There are stars and moving lights,
From airplanes and heavenly sights.

As I drive down this lonely road in the early morn
Daybreak starts to look as if the sky is torn.
Between the darkness of the night,
The brightness of the morning light,
The stars and lights in the sky,
Disappear as if to cry.
Our time is not anymore today,
It is time for us to fade away.
As the sun breaks this early morn,
I drive down this lonely road in the early morn.

Thomas Allen Frith

OH COUNTRY ROAD

Oh country road in need of repair,
Hold your head up and do not despair.
Your arms winds and turns each way,
Up and down hills and past bales of hay.
The trees hang lowly over your head,
Weeds fill in next to your roadbed.

Oh country road in need of repair,
You still have that bright country flair.
Brush and trees grow closely upon your path,
Narrowing your travel area that you hath.
Sometimes your path gets too narrow to travel,
That leaves me to wonder and just marvel.

Oh country road what have you to say?
Wondering if someone will travel you today.
Your road so narrow a car cannot pass,
You had your day of glory in the past.
Your surface being abandoned years ago,
To travel you one has to go so slow.

Oh country road what is thy future,
It has been awhile since your grand statue.
There is not a sign of travels recently,
Maybe it is a sign of the end with decency.
A car has not passed this way in many a day.
Nor will one ever come this way.

ONE NIGHT IN THE COUNTRY

I drive outside this large city,
Feeling a little low and some self-pity.
I decided to head to the country,
To see some sky and some trees.

I head from the city lights,
Planes heading on their flight.
Lights shining from block to block,
Disappear as if a door I unlocked.

Darkness fill in around me,
My vision becomes narrow to see.
I turn down a narrow road,
The type to avoid I have been told.

It was bumpy and very rough,
Making my way a little tough.
At a clearing I decided to stop,
I rolled up the hill to the top.

I look out over the valley below,
Stars shine upon the snow.
It is so quiet I hear the wind talk,
It blows the grassy stalks.

I sit on the hood of my car,
Glazing across the scenery far.
A small house with lights outlining the frame,
Smoke rising from the chimney with no flames.

Scenery of a life that a wish could be,
I watch the smoke rise that I see.
A nippy brisk blows on my neck,
As if a bird flew down and gave a peck.

A spreading chill runs down my arms,
I feel but there is no harm.
Stars shining in the sky high above,
Flicker in the air like a flock of doves.

The wind blows once again,
Giving me a chill and a small pain.
I spend many an hour sitting there alone,
Knowing I must go and return home.

THE HILL

I wander down the hill,
Do I have what it takes and the will?
To get back up once I get down,
Not to have a silly frown.
I get to the bottom of the hill,
I roam around and I mill.
I look back up to the top,
Knowing when I get there I will flop.
I delay my start up that ramp,
The night's air starts to get damp,
I know I must start up that trek,
Knowing when I get to the top I will be a wreck.
I place one foot in front of the other,
Knowing what is ahead makes me shutter.
One step, two step, and then there were three,
Can I make it with this knee?
I continued on the upward path,
Knowing if I don't I will get the wrath.
From being out so very long,
Even though no one knew I was gone.

Thomas Allen Frith

TWO CEDAR TREES

Two cedar trees standing big and tall,
Does anyone notice you anytime at all?
Guarding over the land and area plot.
Does anyone care about you or not?
You can be seen as one approaches your feet,
Many a person there will meet.
You mark the spot for someone dear.
Do they approach you with any fear?
Your position marks a spot so small,
A collection of leaves that does fall.
You provide a good resting place,
A cool shade giving your grace.
The years go galloping by,
Many passed your feet and give a sigh.
You provide that distance mark,
Your age begins to show in your bark.
Will you stand for all the time?
So many can use you to find.
A cool resting place at your feet,
That makes their visit whole and complete.

PATH

I head down the winding path,
Covered by nature's warm bath.
A little slippery on the downward track,
Leaving footprints as I look back.

I travel the path with a task,
Heading nowhere really fast.
To a unknown near destination,
Doing a little exploration.

Raindrops hang on the edge,
Of the lining green hedge.
Brushing against my pants leg,
To ask for help and to beg.

I hear the roar of thunder far;
With knowledge comes ajar.
That another storm is to return,
If nature has not a yearn.

I hasten along the path to the right,
Trying to get home before night.
Trying to beat the storm I hear,
Over my shoulder I do peer.

I want to beat the sight I see,
That wet is a possibility.
I arrive in time right before,
Rain starts as I head in my door.

WALKING TO MIDNIGHT

I walk along the road,
On a very windy night of cold.
I walk down the narrow lane,
Knowing that I must be insane.
To be out here so late at night,
I turn looking in my sight.
Snow floating lazily down,
Brings a smile, not a frown.
I take a step and hear the crunch,
Of limbs on the ground in a bunch.
The wind blows with a chill,
As I top the small little hill.
Why am I out here walking all alone?
Wondering where I do belong.
A clear night sky up in the air,
Bright full moon is sitting there.
What time is it? I ask myself.
Realizing my watch is home on the shelf.
I know it getting very late,
Why am I here, what is my fate?
I see a light ahead of me,
I increase my pace, towards it I flee.
The light does not seem to near,
In fact it is getting less clear.
Around the bend I hear a car,
Seeing it come from afar.

It stops, a person asks me why I am here.
I said I'd rather not be here, but there.
I ask him if he knows the time,
He tells me that it will be fine.
I am out here oh so late,
He said he knows my very fate.
He tells what time it was that night.
I find I was walking to midnight.

Thomas Allen Frith

BIG OAK TREE

The big oak tree sitting gallantly in the yard,
Had your time and it must have been hard.
How old are you? You must have seen,
Many generations since you are so keen.
Your branches hang big and low,
Which are geared to be all so slow.
Children climb the branches so thin,
A tree house, a ladder, a birdhouse and then.
Swings were placed across a branch,
You didn't complain or even give a flinch.
So many people have seen you grow,
So many tales that only you know.
We always wonder how old are you,
Always guessing but never knew.
Twenty, Forty, Eighty years or more,
Never will we know but just adore.
Your stature and your majestic sight,
You stand every day and night.
Everyone asks how old are you,
You will not tell us, we wish we knew.
We try to measure and guess your age,
The results make us very amazed.
You must be older than anyone knows,
We cannot tell as your sap still flows.
How many more years will it be,
For you to be my favorite tree?
I know a tree cannot last forever,
If I could our friendship will not sever.
I notice you're getting tired with age,
I hope to keep seeing you and being amazed.

LITTLE TREE

Little tree so young and small,
You stand so straight and tall.
You have so many years to grow,
If you are not stunted by the snow.
The wind blows your branches so much,
Sometimes I wonder how you can take it such.
You look so frail just standing there,
With your leaves waving like hair.
The robin upon your branch did light,
To take a rest from its daily flight.
There is the blue bird flying by,
Darting above you in the sky.
Oh little tree will once be big,
Grown from a small oak twig.

Thomas Allen Frith

COUNTRY CHURCH

There is that lonely country church
Sitting by the road,
It has a long and interesting history
That I am told.

It sits silently and lonely there beneath
The tall bushy pine trees.
As I look around and a sight I see
Busy little honey bees.

Why would anyone want to resign
On such a site?
I guess that was their decision
It was their right.

To close such a beautiful place
That used to be,
On Sunday visiting the Lord
Praising with glee.

I stare in a daze as it sits there
All alone and quite.
There is nothing I can do
Even in spite,

To help this place build to return
To its fullest glory,
Continue to be a living historical
And emotional story.

I decide to go and check out
The one that bought,
The building I love
The one I sought.

I discovered that
The one who bought
Made my worries
For all the naught.

OLD COUNTRY ROAD

Old country road winding and lonesome as can be,
Winding aimlessly throughout the country as you only know.
Where you go, one has to wait in order to see,
When one dares to travel they must move carefully and go slow.

You have been neglected far from your best days,
Old country road once used by many going to and fro.
They traveled your long winding path, each going their way,
They used you proudly traveling to market or to work as they go.

The years have left you lonely as people have moved away,
As those few that remained most dearly has been left to know.
Old country road stay proud and hold your head, do not sway.
I know the holes that wear on your surface must pain you so.

Don't let anyone take away your pride or let out a sigh,
You know you served us well as history will be told.
We all will remember your glory days and try not to cry,
As you stay firm in your objective to be bold.

Old country road can you see what is beginning to happen
People are moving back and will need you services once again.
We will take the time to remember the way you were then,
Refreshing your worn and aching body, a freshness to be obtain.

You waited for years sobbing and knowing it was going to be,
Old country road we are here to keep your glory flowing.
Forgive us of our total neglect, the future we did not see,
But old country road we will keep your face glowing

WHAT I SAW

There jumps a fish upon the lake,
It looks as if the scenery is all a fake.
Did I see the fish as I thought had?
Did I have a dream that was bad?
I heard the water as it splashed,
Saw the ripples as it mashed.
What did I really see that day?
I do not know or do I want to say.
I didn't see anything at all,
Maybe I did if I could recall.
I think about what I saw,
I sit and become a little awe.
I tell myself I did see,
I must go, away I flee.
The more I think about it today,
I will have something to say.
I saw a fish jump across the lake,
I know what I saw was fake.
What did I see that moment I heard?
Maybe it was just a big diving bird.
Swooping down to grab that fish,
The one I saw or that I wish.

FISHING

The day is bright and the weather clear,
I feel, ache, and a calling I hear.
I gather my stuff and begin to head out,
I am on a mission, which is no doubt.
I cross the high grassy wide meadow,
Which I have seen from my window.
Across another meadow I do cross,
I am on a mission no matter the cost.
Up a bank, some water I do spy,
Shining brightly and reflecting the sky.
Smooth clear water with some lily pads,
A scene I have seen many times with my dad.
I empty my hands and begin to prepare,
While watching the sun and feeling the air.
A tree I spy off to one side,
A place I can rest from the sun, I hide.
I select my place under the tree,
Let me rest and let me be.
I take my line and swing it in,
A splash I hear as I set my pin.
I set my place and begin to dream,
I can accomplish what I deem.
I rest my body on the ground,
And wait until a fish I have found.
I am set for a day of lazy fishing,
Till the sun sets and begins to be missing.
I don't care if a fish is caught,
I had this day that I had sought.
Back home I head with the days catch,
For a night rest I do fetch.

Family

HAPPY ANNIVERSARY

Happy Anniversary to you my dear,
Something I know you love to hear.
It is two words that means much,
Special meaning and special touch.
Forgive me for not saying them each year,
Darling, you know I love you dear.
If I fail to say them sincerely to you,
You know I meant them, yes I do.
I may not be as sentimental as I should,
Let me say this if I could.
I love dearly each and every day,
You know that without a word I say.
I may not utter these words my dear,
My actions and deeds will let you hear.
Happy anniversary to you my sweet,
Honey you are one no one can beat.
I love you more than just words,
They are words, with meaning not blurred.
I do not want to create any adversity,
Honey let me say, Happy Anniversary.

Thomas Allen Frith

MY DAD

He was involved with us many a time,
Even when good times were hard to find.
A farmer at first, a tenet at that;
I remember that big straw hat.

Times he spent in the fields,
Always working on making a deal.
Year after year he labored hard,
Watching the weather and being on guard.

Years of trying to get the crops in,
Carrying cotton to the nearest gin.
It seems that there was never an end,
To our whines he did not bend.

Years past by unable to gain ground,
A new job and living place was found.
Many an odd job he did try to do,
Making sure we had something to wear to school.

An opportunity did once come about,
I know there was never a second doubt.
To take the challenge and move again,
On a new career he headed off to begin.

To add to his interest he learned a pastime,
Repairing televisions and radios and painted a sign.
I helped at times and learned from him,
Little bit here but filling my brim.

He was there for us day by day,
The three of us grew up and went out way.
Retirement came and he moved back home,
Back to where he raised us and where we roamed.

He did his fishing and gardening on his time,
Looking for a new craft he always did fine.
Each year at Christmas we would gather with him,
A gift of love, a calendar and a tree well-trimmed.

Then on one Christmas, a tragedy was not planned.
As we review his total lifespan.
It was many a sad day to sigh,
He left us and went to live with God on high.

We were not ready for him to leave us,
We have to accept it, yes we must.
Days past and many are sad,
I will always love and remember my dad.

Thomas Allen Frith

MY MOM

She was there each and every day,
We went along our own way.
Always caring and helping our hurts,
Trying to keep us in clothes in our growing spurts.

She might have made mistakes but did not we care,
Not as long as her love was there.
Many a memory is etched in our minds,
And not a better mom could one find.

A picnic in the pasture we had one summer day,
She did her best and let us play.
Always encouraged us to improve our education,
Expanding our knowledge and imagination.

If one was ill or not feeling good,
She took the time and did the best she could.
She never criticized nor put one down,
She never caused us to wear a frown.

During the time she worked outside,
She never let an opportunity pass by.
Many days she came home tired and frayed,
Never complained not even to this day.

She spent much time looking after our dad,
When he passed she was very sad.
Strong was she when things went not her way,
No bad things would you hear her say.

There was no cool air when it was hot
A complaint from her you would hear not.
She stayed by dad in his last days,
Lead us even though she had no say.

Mom wanted all the best for us,
She would never let us fuss.
One day her youngest son past on,
Knowing that two of her loved ones were gone.

She held her head up and kept us on track,
We knew she would always look back.
Memories of the days that we all played,
When we were all together on special days.

Now days have passed slow and all along,
Since the good days of the past are gone.
She sets her mind on firm ground,
Never a better mom can be found.

Thomas Allen Frith

MY WIFE

My wife I love and adore so much,
Sometimes take her for granted and such.
How can I treat her the way I do,
When she cares for me when I have the flu?

I do not say I love you enough,
It is hard to say, sometimes tough.
I do not know why it is so,
I love her more than she knows.

I wonder to myself so many times,
Of the one the Lord helped me find.
I love her is what I need to say,
For her to hear it each and every day.

Why do I not say it as she likes to hear?
I love her so much and so dear.
I think about her every day and night,
And even if we were to fight.

I can only say I will love her forever,
Our love never be one to sever.
My wife I love how do I show?
Maybe to carry her across some deep snow?

Maybe a surprise every once and a while,
And of course every time I look at our child.
She would love to hear me say,
"I love you," each and every day.

Can I find a way to express my thoughts?
Maybe a surprise or a gift I bought.
Why do I not show her love as much,
As she thinks others do as such?

I do little things that means a lot to me,
It's not enough for her to see.
I surprise her by little things I do,
Instead I wish I would say I love you..

For me it is not my way,
To say I love you each and every day.
If I fail to say I love you dear,
At least I would like to hold you near.

In my mind I always plan,
To say I love you and let it stand.
Although I fail to say to you,
I really do. I do love you.

DADDY

Daddy, Daddy oh dear dad,
Sometimes he made me happy as well as sad.
How can I remember all the events?
There was that time with the tent.

How about the time in the swimming hole,
He tried to teach me to swim in the cold.
How about the time I traced his steps?
The attention he gave when he tried to help.

There is the time that I was crushed,
To me he hurried and fast he rushed.
Busy was he in providing for all of us,
In doing so, we never heard a fuss.

Did I do all the things he wished me to do?
Maybe I did except one or two.
I made mistakes as time went on,
He knew I would and they I own.

I knew I was extending my life,
As I left home and took a wife.
He never said if I was right or wrong,
He knew life would continue to go on.

He took her in as if his own,
He knew we were all grown.
Years went past and busy I got,
I love him still and forgot him not.

When his time on earth came to an end,
I knew I was forever losing a friend.
It was hard for me to say goodbye,
I tried very hard not to cry.

I must say that I could not do,
Many like him are very few.
I felt a closeness that one night,
I cried and thought of his flight.

I will miss him so much as time goes by,
Dad, I know you know that I cried.
Time goes on forever without him,
I will and I do without a whim.

I spend my time here on earth,
Waiting to see you with my rebirth.
Daddy, daddy, oh dear dad,
I will survive but he knows I am sad.

Thomas Allen Frith

MY SPECIAL ANGEL

I have one that I care so much about,
People would wonder though if I shout.
You mean so much to me this day,
I do not know how to say.

I love you or I care so very much,
Should it be something else as such.
I have lived my life each day for you,
I have made my life as I do.

I try to figure what I will do,
I try to express this to you.
I know you are the love of my life,
You have been for years, my wife.

I try to think of that special name,
Maybe a relative or someone of fame.
With smile and a glee,
My Special Angel it will be.

Maybe not an angel that we all recall,
One to love and one I cannot deny at all.
To guide me and mold me each day,
While we work and have fun at play.

I want to call you by your name,
You may think it is just a game.
You make everything around me gel,
You are my loving and Special Angel.

MY BROTHER

My brother, my brother, Oh why was it you?
I don't understand why but I will have to make do.
You were the youngest and last it would be,
No matter what I think I will have to see.
The decision to leave was not made by you,
I will have to accept that and make do.
I say good bye to you today,
I have no choice what else can I say.

My brother, my brother, Oh why was it you?
We had fun but this day was the day for you.
If I could, I would try to have my way,
You looked at me and I could hear you say,
Don't worry about me for I will be fine,
Be yourself and treat everybody kind.
I looked at you one last time,
I knew that I would have to resign.

My brother, my brother, Oh why was it you?
Now you are gone everybody will be blue.
Memories are there for us to recall,
We will stand so proudly and tall.
To tell everybody we knew you so,
We know that we have to let you go.
Each of us will remember and make do,
My brother, my brother why was it you?

MY SPECIAL WIFE

I met you on that special day,
You said I did not have much to say.
It was lunch, we shared the time,
I did not know you would be mine.

Days past before I knew,
That you were special and one of few.
The days past we knew not,
That together we would live, each we got.

Love grew so fast for us,
Many adjustments that was a must.
Time takes its pace as we moved on,
Letting the past leave and be gone.

You made me special as I did you,
We shared our lives, the days were few.
Love grew each and every day,
I still did not have much to say.

Days passed as we grew nearer,
Our time became special and dearer.
Without you I could not live,
My love to you I give.

My special wife you would be,
All the people will stare and see.
We are one and always will be,
As we go each day with a glee.

Our future is ours as we make each day,
I begin to learn more to say.
Tomorrow is better than yesterday
Our love grows and more I say.

Years will pass faster than we want,
My love will not waiver, no it won't.
I look at your each and every day,
I will always love you as I turn all gray.

Each day with you is so fabulous,
Our time will be ours with love and trust.
I love you until that final end,
Even then, the end I will try to bend.

I love you, my special wife,
To be with you all my life
I will not look back to regret
That day in the restaurant where we met.

Thomas Allen Frith

THREE YOUNG BOYS

Three young boys, a mischievous as can be,
Was a challenge for mom as most could see.
They gave her good times as well as bad,
They did some things that made her mad.
Although they did the things they had done,
Mom still loved them and enjoyed the fun.

As they grew up and went their way,
Always telling her they would return one day.
The fast and busy pace that they lived,
They love her much, that they will give.
The days flew by in a hasty pace,
They lived in the modern human race.

One day as in great totality,
The three boys had to face reality.
A father's good health was fading away,
The younger was limited in his days.
What could they do to help each out?
Sometimes all that was left was to shout.

On a calm and quiet December day,
Their dad passed on and went his way.
It wouldn't be long before they knew,
That little brother's life was through.
Now the three brothers remain as two
Not knowing exactly what to do.

Would it be the older or the next,
That would make the world complex?
Which one would be the next in line?
They all knew it is a matter of time.
Three young boys no more to be,
Until all of them are in eternity.

KEVIN

Keep me in the forefront of your mind.
Every good thought I hope will be ours to find.
Very few times we will cross our paths;
I am one, your father's better half;
Now as in my life, you will be in mine.

Remember your dad as age becomes to be,
Always we will share and always we will see.
You are important, from us do not flee.

KARI

Keep the smile and happiness you have shown,
Always remember I am here and now on my own.
Reach out at any time and we will share;
Inside me you are important and I hope you care.

Reach out to me when you need some help;
Each time you need secrets to be kept.
Never will I forsake you in your family's life;
Every time you have a need or have any strife,
Encircle me as part of you and your family's life.

SHEREE

Soundly you accept me in your mother's new life.
How can I be accepted in yours without any strife?
Every moment you will be important to me.
Rather than resentment I want us to care and see,
Each memory that is created will be important for you,
Every day you will receive my love that you are due.

TAMMY

Today your parents will begin to share the rest of their life;
Adventures to share as we are husband and wife.
Moments we will have and a lifetime to explore;
Memories for all of us to cherish as life will afford.
You will always be a part of our family life.

Join with us as we travel our future path,
Every moment will count, you figure the math;
A life forever in love and that is a must.
Never to worry, we are here to trust.

WIFE

She is a woman all her own,
May have many gripes and moans.
She starts each day in a run,
Finishes it without all being done.
She does everything she could possibly do,
Even when feeling bad and having the flu.
She puts her family first in her life,
Seems to take it all without any strife.
There is cooking, cleaning and job too,
She handles it all when even feeling blue.
She raises her children along the way,
She does not care what others have to say.
She is always there for me,
Even with the time I could not see.
She treats my scrapes and injuries too,
She is not a nurse, she knows what to do.
I met this wonderful person some time ago,
That is another story yet to be told.
She will give me all her adult life,
I love her and made her my loving wife.

Home

FOUR WALLS

Four walls I see around me today,
There is nothing to do nor to say.
I stay my time inside this place,
I do not see another's face.
Alone am I inside these walls,
They grow narrow and tall.
There seems to be no escape,
I grab a roll of tape.
Why do I do this you may ask?
Why would I go to such a task?
I use the tape to selectively judge,
The sunlight moving with a gentle nudge.
For you see if the sun does not shine,
I know the day is left behind.
As long as I see the sun on the tape,
I know from these walls I cannot escape.
Four wall holds me from within,
Is this a prison or a restrictive pen?
I sit viewing the cold four walls,
Waiting for my mother to gently call.
"It is time to eat and your penalty is done."
I can escape these walls and have some fun.

LONELY CHAIR

I sit and watch the lonely chair,
I see it sitting lonesome over there.
No one is showing it any personal attention,
Not any desire, or showing any affection.
The chair sits there oh so very still.
No one seems to be making it a big deal.
Lonely, still, and not making a sound,
Although people travel about and all around.
No one seems to want to sit,
Not even give it attention a little bit.
No one looks upon its lonely sight,
Not even looking left or right.
Someone pulls it silently away,
To be used another day.

CLOCK

Tick, Tock, Tick, Tock,
Goes the sound of the clock.
Bong, Bong, Bong, and another Bong.
Four O'clock is its song.

Tick, Tock, Tick, Tock,
Goes the sound of the clock.
I take a glance at its lonely face,
Listen to the sound of its pace.

Tick, Tock, Tick, Tock,
Goes the sound of the clock.
Was I wrong at the time I saw?
Time is moving so slow I am appalled.

Tick, Tock, Tick, Tock,
Goes the sound of the clock.
Forget the time I tell myself,
The sound is making me deaf.

Thomas Allen Frith

A ROOMFUL OF ROSES

A roomful of roses I would give to you,
For putting up with me and paying your dues.
We have been through many events,
Never complaining or giving a hint.

A roomful of roses I would give to you,
As I moved and you went too.
Where ever we did go for a small time,
Many enjoyable times we did find.

A roomful of roses I would give to you,
For loving me and putting up with the things I do.
We may move to Arizona or Illinois,
You didn't like it but, you kept your poise.

A roomful of roses I would give to you,
We settled for a while, if we only knew,
What would be the total experience?
A small delay, a hindrance.

A roomful of roses I would give to you,
You put up with me and paid your dues.
We returned to the area we were raised,
Always saying and giving it a praise.

A roomful of roses I would give to you,
One day we would move you always knew.
We desired to move and lived in one place,
Until we did, you always kept you face.

A roomful of roses I would give to you.
That would not be enough if I do.
You deserve more than a full room,
To put up with a life of your loving groom.

HOME

Home is where I always will be,
Not a house or up in a tree.
It is where as a young boy I had,
A nice, warm, and safe night bed.

Home is not where I am at,
A place to hang my coat and hat.
It is where my mother did care;
Where I watched and nightly stared.

Home can be any place at all,
It can be a place that we so call.
Home at the end of the day,
Where we hang our head, talk and say.

It is not just a resting place,
It has spirit and love and many a face.
Home is what loved ones makes it to be,
Each does give their loving deeds.

A caring parent one or two;
Makes me wondering just what to do.
Home can be in the past,
Memories of love that inside will last.

Home may be with my family tonight,
Maybe new or old to one sight.
Home is where I want to be
With the loves I know and I want to see.

PICTURES ON THE WALL

Pictures on the wall,
With memories to recall.
Memories all are past,
Not one second to last.
A snapshot of history,
A past loving memory.

A mental image of the event,
So a copy can be sent.
To relatives of the ones not there,
To those who wish to care.
A picture of the precious moment,
A memory to have a comment.

I wish I was there,
To have a witness to bear.
That the moment is all past,
With no way to make it last.
Except in a picture on the wall,
With memories to recall.

Thomas Allen Frith

THE WALL

Look upon the wall there nearby,
Tell me what you see or spy.
A picture, a plaque, or a clock,
Attached itself as if to mock.
Staring down upon this place,
As if there were a glaring face.

Why are they there and why that wall?
Do they have a special call?
They were put there by someone's hand,
To display a message and to take a stand.
The face of the clock keeps moving about,
And the picture just seems to shout.

They are here for the owner's desire,
They hang lazily by the open fire.
There is a purpose to place them here,
It makes us shine and seems to appear.
That the reason they are here in their place,
Is each of them has a face.

To display for others to see this day,
They come and go along the way.
Look upon the wall there nearby,
Smile, or cry, let out a sigh.
For you see the reason they are here,
Is to remember someone that we hold dear.

PENALTY

Seven o'clock, Eight o'clock oh what time is it?
I wait and wait, here as I sit.
It has to be much later than that,
I know because of how long I have sat.

Nine o'clock or maybe even ten,
I look at the clock once again.
I do not know what time it may be,
I sit here and look trying to see.

The clock is hidden from my sight,
Is it over on my right?
I seek and search for the actual time,
To no avail as I lose my prime.

I sit here growing old as I look,
I turn my head and give it a crook.
Trying to stretch it to my left,
I cannot keep control of myself.

"What time is it?" I finally ask,
As if it was a major task.
The response I did not want to hear,
For it starts with "Do not worry dear,"

The next part of what I do hear,
It is what I thought and actually fear.
"Your time is not over for a while,"
The words came with a smile.

Thomas Allen Frith

My mother said these very words to me,
For the time I wish I could see.
She added to them with a calm reply,
It made me react with a long sigh.

For my penalty that was applied,
For something that I wish I could have died.
I broke the rules that I must live by,
So now I sit and cry and cry.

THE PICTURE

The picture on the wall,
Sitting lonely and hanging still.
Has memories that we recall,
To some that makes a big deal.

The picture of a loved one,
At an age that will not return.
Events where we had fun,
One picture we had a concern.

The picture of the past,
Showing styles that has faded away.
Some of the forgotten tasks,
That we did on that memorable day.

The picture some people ask about,
Why we would take such a snap.
While one was fishing for trout,
It landed in his lap.

That picture was a moment in time,
To enjoy each and every day.
Knowing that it again will never find,
As we travel on life's way.

Thomas Allen Frith

TELEPHONE CALL

Ring, Ring, Ring and another Ring,
What is that noise or that thing?
It interrupts my sleep that is so sound,
I wake up and start to frown.
Who would be calling this time of night?
I realize it might cause me fright.
I turn and try to answer the call,
I hear the clock as it falls.
I search for the telephone in the dark,
I reach and again miss the mark.
Where is that thing? I know it is there,
The next noise I am not prepared.
There goes the glass I placed by the phone,
If I do not hurry they will think nobody's home.

Ring, Ring, Ring and another Ring,
It seems to make noise and start to sing.
Once again I reach and come up short,
Now I am beginning to get a little tort.
I cannot find it even though it is there,
I reach again and come up with air.
With all the tries I am now wide awake,
Realizing it is already daybreak.
I turn and finally I do find,
The telephone with its cords in a bind.
The cords I try to untangle speedy and fast,
I knew this call may become one of the past.
I answer hello as to my ear I do cup,
There is no voice because they hung up.

I READ A BOOK

I read a book the other day,
A special message it had to say.
I read it without putting it down,
Or even displaying a worry frown.
I read the book from front to back,
Interest and attention it did not lack.
The book I picked once again,
I opened the covers and I begin.
To read its story page by page,
My interest it captured in a cage.
Why is this book so capturing?
What do I care as I start reading?

Thomas Allen Frith

THE BOOK

There is a book I am told to read,
For me it will be a struggle, a task indeed.
The book looks large with very small print,
Oh to read this will be quite a stink.

I scan the pages as if to see,
To get an idea how long it will take me.
I gently open the pages and give it a good look,
Oh, if I could have already read this book.

I start to read trying to get involved,
As if it was a mystery to be solved.
The words caught my eyes and hooked me in,
I read with intent as if there were no end.

For you see the book I feared at first,
Captured my attention and made me thirst.
To read a book that was well written,
Was worth the effort and praise I given.

THE CHAIR

The chair sits lonely on the floor,
Over by the window near the door.
It sits there facing the rest of the room,
It looks so burdened with gloom.

Does it feel ignored or is it to be,
An ornament made from a tree?
Does anyone care how it feels,
We may need to get actually real.

Can a chair feel or have emotion too?
Can it get sad and feel real blue?
No one means to pass it by,
The neglect makes it want to cry.

Someone sits as they walk by,
I know I heard a silent sigh.
Someone finally took some care,
As now the chair feels like a chair.

Thomas Allen Frith

THE HALL

I walk down the long narrow hall,
I had to be careful and try not to fall.
The floor was wet and had not dried yet,
I know I will make someone mad I bet.

I turn and look straight behind me,
A set of footprints as far as I can see.
Should I have waited to walk this way?
Maybe tomorrow or later today?

Do I continue down the long hall?
Do I dare to turn around at all?
The decision I make is to be,
To continue down the hall and hope no one sees.

THE MIRROR

Mirror there on the wall,
I think I have heard this as I recall.
What is the image that I kindly see,
Staring and looking back at me?

Is it someone that I know tonight?
The image is giving me a small fright.
Who is the person I so attentively view?
Is it one that has already paid his dues?

It looks like someone other than I
Is it someone there to watch or spy?
Who is the person I ask inside?
I know its identity cannot hide.

I look real close into the eyes,
Oh me oh my oh me oh my,
How can this be me as I see,
A person grown up? I try to flee,

It's no use trying to hide,
It is me actually that is inside.
Can I accept this new gained knowledge?
I walk away with a new found courage

Thomas Allen Frith

THE PICTURE ON THE WALL

The picture on the wall sitting there so still,
I wonder who the people are and always will.
They face the room so bold and tall,
Does anyone know them at all?

One person two then three or four,
Posing so beautiful for all to adore.
Each has their smile upon their face,
Hanging on the wall in their place.

A visitor looks and politely asks,
Who is that person under the glass?
Someone says I think I know,
Yet my memory is so slow.

Maybe it's someone that I recall
From my childhood when I was small.
It is a relative of mine,
In my memory I cannot find

The name of the two in the back,
The ones in front my memory lack.
Maybe 1 should really recall,
I just don't know any at all.

THE REMOTE

What can be said about a TV remote?
An instrument that makes a man gloat.
What is this piece of plastic we see,
That makes men and women such enemies?
Men use it to scan the channels,
Women wish it hung like a wall panel.
Men say it gives him freedom,
From lousy shows and the boredom.
Women say destroy it please.
It is only used as a tease.
Men see it as a way to scan.
Women see the image of a frying pan.
Men push each and every button.
Women think that it is his big glutton.
For what a toy to play for free,
Women see as a monstrosity.
Put that remote down this very minute,
Yell women as they get fed up with it.
Men indicate he does not understand.
I am just trying to see what I can.
Men comply and put it down,
Later pick it up and start another round.

WALLS

There is a wall to my right,
One on my left in sight.
There is one in front well as one behind.
I wonder to myself as I try to find
A wall that will talk to me.
Can they talk and even see?
If they could what would they say?
I wish they would and yet they may.
I scan their face well adorned,
With pictures of the past all worn.
I notice what there is to see,
The picture of someone maybe me.
There are others attached to each wall,
Memories each brings and makes me recall.
Yes, they help me as I finally see,
I am the one, as the walls analyze me.

WINDOW

The window sits there for me to see,
Looking outside and wanting to flee.
Out the window I look at the sight,
I am glad it is not night.
I see the yard with people there,
Rushing by, not knowing where.
The window provides with a glance,
The butterflies doing their dance.
It allows a clear view for one to see,
The robin singing loudly with glee.
I notice a friend traveling nearby,
He races on his feet and passes by.
I notice the birds building their nest,
Taking a much needed rest.

The trees are green with fresh leaves,
There within as the air gives heaves.
The ants and bees that amble by,
If strung would make me cry.
There is that crawling worm,
The looks of it makes my wife squirm.
What about the grass and the weeds?
I knew I should have planted the new seeds.
The flowers growing in glory delight,
Only to close as it get near night.
The sun gently fades away,
I leave the window for another day.

Animals

MY DOG

Many a time I take a walk,
With my dog as I talk.
He is my friend, knows me well,
We travel the hills and dales.
I share my thoughts with him each day,
There is nothing I would not say.
Many a thing we tried,
Together we did with our pride.
I run. I walk. He does the same.
He is smart and not at all lame.
He wonders around as we travel about,
Returns to me, if I were to shout.
He is my friend I can depend,
Never away I would I ever send.
He laughs at me as we do play,
He barks back at me as to say;
Everything is fun and very fine,
He is my dog and only mine.
My dog and I walked today,
We go about and on our way.
You will always find him with me,
We are together and enjoy with glee.
Never apart people knew dear,
If we were there or even here.
One day he went away,
I did not know where nor could not say.
Many a year before I knew why
He had passed away, and to this day I still cry.

Thomas Allen Frith

THERE LIES A CAT

There lies a cat so peaceful and sound,
If you look at him he has a frown.
He lies there taking his morning nap,
Up in the middle of my comfortable warm lap.

There lies a cat so peaceful and proud,
To be loved and away from the crowd.
He has no worries and know it is so,
He doesn't have to stay out in the snow.

There lies a cat being so very lazy,
He lies there thinking others are crazy;
Of the fuss they make over him lying there,
They act like children young and fair.

There lies a cat so peaceful and uncaring,
Actually sleeping and does a little snoring.
He lies there with his head turned up,
Which would be better a cat or a pup?

There lies a cat so peaceful and quiet,
He is so smart and very bright.
He knows that his life is so unmatched,
As those cats that are unattached.

So you see this cat has it made,
Each and every night and day;
He doesn't have to get down,
Since he is laying there peaceful and sound.

HOOT, HOOT

Hoot, Hoot, and another Hoot I hear.
I can make it out loud and clear.
I love the sound I hear this day,
That comes from not far away.

Hoot, Hoot, and another Hoot I hear.
The sound I love and is so dear.
I do not get to see you this day,
You leave and go on your way.

Hoot, Hoot, I hear across the dell.
I can't quite hear so I yell.
"Hurry back some other day,
I wish to visit if I may."

MR. COYOTE

Mr. Coyote running across the field,
Why is everybody making such a big deal?
You are on your way home after a night of work,
To your cozy little home while there is a little dark.
You run fast across the dry prairie grass,
You carry your head with that proud coyote class.
Dodge behind a hill along the way,
Behind a barn, tree and a pile of hay.
You do not dare to wonder near,
Because there is that human fear.

Someone yells "go get my gun."
You know that it is not just for fun.
You hurry along at a faster pace,
The hunter you do not want to face.
You hurry along your way,
There breaks a new and beautiful day.
Daylight peeks on the near horizon,
A face that is the bright round sun.
It lifts rapidly into the morning air,
You dash home with your beastly flare.

It doesn't take you long to disappear,
To hear the people breathe a relief from fear.
Knowing you have gone and left them alone,
That you have left and away you have gone.
There is the talk of seeing you that day,
Oh what terrible things they say.
About the fears they have of you,
There is nothing that you can do.
Mr. Coyote you have gone on your way
Maybe I will see you another day.

Thomas Allen Frith

MR. WOODPECKER

Hello, Mr. Woodpecker with your head so red,
As you peck upon the tree that is dead.
Ratta tat tat Ratta tat tat.
As if to say, "Here take that."
I feed you your favorite food.
Time passes as I watch and I stood.

Watching you as you go your separate way,
As you fly I just had to say,
"Hurry back for another meal"
I like to visit with you as you are so real.
Hurry back and I will have more for you.
I will have what you want and are due.

Your red head bobbing to and fro,
As you eat precise and slow.
I know you are out to get,
A worm or something good I bet.
Do I hear you off oh so far?
Your sound is drowned out by a car.

You move on to a tree across the way,
Not being able to hear what I have to say.
I will provide you with all the food you will need,
If you will listen to me and just heed.
I enjoy the times we have together,
Knowing I will make your life a little better.

MY CATS

I watch my pet sleep on the floor,
I watch him over by the door.
He is so peaceful lying there,
With his long and shiny hair.

I want to go over and play with him,
I do then I notice two of them.
How could I forgot about my second pet?
I love them both this I bet.

The other one walks sneaking by,
Turns and looks at me and sighs.
Why is the first so sound asleep,
Lying there and not making a peep?

The second one wonder over by him.
Stops and looks, as I call "NO, JIM."
It is too late; for there he trounced,
Upon the first and landed with a bounce.

Right in the middle of the first one there,
With no graciousness nor flare.
Landed right in the middle of him,
As I said, "Oh poor Slim."

The two of them started their fight,
The first swatted and then took flight.
The second raced behind as if to grin,
Chased him around and around and back again.

They raced throughout the room,
While my mom went to get the broom.
I told her, "No let them play,
They do this every day."

Slim and Jim may have their fun,
They chase each other as they run.
They finish their task of the day,
It is now time to nap and hit the hay.

They lay there by the door,
They sleep and I hear them snore.
They are quite and silent into the night,
Both of my cats lay there in my sight.

A PET

A pet is one that I love so dear.
It has love and nothing to fear.
Why does a pet need to worry;
About a meal or a bone to bury?

A pet is one to keep me company,
To lay and sleep under the canopy.
It is there to love and to protect,
Gives me attention and much respect.

A pet is one that I look daily for;
Lying at the door upon the floor.
I come home from being away,
My attention I get without anything to say.

A pet is one that becomes a part of the family,
His actions and stunts I watch in glee.
So amazed that he knows so much,
A trick, a nudge or such and such.

A pet is one that parting hurts each day,
A feeling that one cannot express or say.
I miss him each and every day,
I would have him back if I had my way.

Thomas Allen Frith

THE RABBIT

I saw a rabbit hopping past me the other day,
I ask him if he had anything to say.
He looked at me as if I had gone nuts,
He dashed in the bushes, the kind that cuts.

I watched to see where he tried to go,
I noticed his travel was a little slow.
He made his way through the deep bush,
Off he took in a fast hopping rush.

He stopped to look back at me,
If there was something for him to see.
I kept watching as he hopped along,
It was not long before he was gone.

I started to take off on my way,
Then I noticed he was there as if to say.
"Thank you for looking after me,
As I tried to hurry in my flee.

I took the thorny bush route,
I was able to get through and out.
Thank you for not making me rush,
Through that big thorny bush.

If I had I would certainly be,
Torn and cut that would be me."
I watched him turn and leave,
I do know or at least believe.

He was a friend to be,
As it took one last look at me.
I made a friend that day in the park,
But I must go now because it is dark.

COYOTE

Hey there coyote run fast as you will,
Across the meadow and down the hill.
You're a pest to some,
A friend to none.
Run cautiously hiding along the way,
Knowing you will be back another day.
Where have you been?
What had you seen?
I want to protect all of my pets and things,
From a predator that disaster brings.
Run as you will,
Hurriedly down the hill.
I just hope you are actually passing this way by,
Traveling to another place where to lie.
Run away fast,
For me just pass.

CAT RUBS

The cat rubs upon my legs,
Letting me know and beginning to beg.
I do not know if she is hungry or tired.
I know if I do not pick her up she will be wired.
I reach down to give her a hand,
I reach for her collar and her waist band.
I reach under her belly so fine,
Trying to be nice and kind.
I start to lift her into my arms,
She lets out her terrible alarm.
She jumps through my hands so tight,
Races about with her state of fright.
I missed what she wanted so much,
She just wanted attention and such.
The next time she rubs against me,
I will wait for her as she pleases.
I will let her rub against my legs,
Rise up on her hind legs as she begs.
I will do my daily chores,
Let her rub for now and more.

THE CROW

I wander out into the crisp morning air,
My mind wants to wonder if I dare.
It is still and peaceful as in the night,
The sun rises with it bright sunlight.
There is not a soul around,
Not even an animal can be found.
I am alone with Mother Nature,
I take a step as I begin to venture.
I hear a sound that I recognize,
One that I start to criticize.
The sound echoes and gets louder,
I search and find it over yonder,
A crow sitting high on a wall.
Letting me know he gave me the call.
His caw breaks the morning air,
I glance without despair.
There he sits by himself,
High as if on a shelf.
He sits there all alone,
Later he is gone.
I wonder if he was waiting for me,
To come out and to glance and see,
Him sitting up so high on the wall,
Knowing I could not touch him at all.

Did he call me to show his might?
Was he trying to do it in spite?
Did he know I did not care,
If he was sitting there?
He is gone at this time.
Will he return for me to find,
Him sitting high on the wall,
To give me that morning call?

LOVE

Love is dear, and hard to find,
When you do, it is so kind.
Love grows along the way,
This is what they say.
Love can be happy and sets one free.
It is something that some might want to flee.
Love is not for everyone,
Only you and the one you won.
Love is there for any to grasp,
It is there from the past.
Love can be a blessing for you today,
It can be whatever it may.
Love is not easy to define;
If you find it, it is so fine.

Thomas Allen Frith

ALCAN HIGHWAY

When you begin at Milepost Zero,
You will travel along a road constructed by heroes.
Although the road has changed with time,
A traveler now has sceneries to find.
At Dawson Creek begins this chore,
Then to Ft. Nelson getting the traveler a little bored.
There is the area that is Suicide Hill,
That tested many a man's will.
What about Pink or Trutch Mountain that is not that much,
Toad River and Steamboat is different as such.
There is Muncho Lake that is green as an emerald,
The signposts at Watson Lake is almost a miracle.
There is great ice cream at a stop in Teslin
Staying the night at Whitehorse to a late check-in.
Although there is much more to see,
One that travels knows Dawson City is a place to be.
It is not on the famous road that we travel,
The highway there does give this road a rival.
To the south is the famous town of Skagway,
It is a diversion and out of the way.
Back on the road again heading west,
We try to travel and progress at best.
At Haines Junction we head to the north,
With several freeze heaves that's nothing to scarf.
Past Soldier Summit and on to Destruction Bay,
The history and stories they have to say.

We reach the Canadian town of Beaver Creek,
Our car has been shook and begin to creak.
We cross back into our country of origin,
The state of Alaska is to begin.
An adventure that one does not know,
Unless one has visited this state where the wind thus blow.
Watching the fox race across in front of us,
It removes the boredom and the fuss.
We move into the small town of Tok,
Hoping the prices here will not get us broke.
With Delta Junction ahead to finish this trek,
From here to there and back to Dawson Creek.

Thomas Allen Frith

LOVE SO FINE

When does it begin, love that is so fine?
Maybe on the day that we first met.
Love is for all and not just mine,
Each will share it, that I bet.

Love grows fonder over the years,
You must work with it for it to stay.
There will be happiness and many a tear,
As each mold their love removing their fear.

When did it begin? I still ask inside,
Does it matter as long as it is there?
There is no way to cover it or try to hide,
There is that smile and outside flair.

When did it begin? I try to recall.
I remember the fun that we had.
The beginning doesn't matter if it is not at all,
When it gone it makes life bad.

When our time together is separated by fate,
I will feel sorrow and more than that.
I will remember that first date,
Wonder why it had to end and where love is at.

The day that love leaves me will be the day you are gone
It will be the worst day of my life.
Knowing it is not there and has to pass on.
I will still love you and take each day in strife.

ALL ALONE

All alone I seem to be,
No one around that I see.
I sit down by myself,
Listening as if I am deaf.
I sit in the room so bare,
Wondering if I am really there.
Is there one next to me,
Maybe to one I could plea.
I feel I am there all alone,
As the minutes and hours are gone.
I know I am there, just me,
No one is there to see.

All alone and wondering why,
As time continues to pass me by.
I wish I knew why here I am,
Maybe it is unreal or just a scam.
There are no doors for me to leave,
An exit is there, that I believe.
No windows are on the wall I see,
Maybe if there was I would flee.
I am here all alone,
But then the image is gone.
It is a wonder or so it seems,
Because it was all in a night's dream.

FALLING AGAIN

Throughout the years I have had many a fall,
None serious or injury at all.
I have tripped over my own feet,
My balance has put me on my seat.
There is that nasty fall,
I do not know how it happened at all.
I find myself on the ground
No reason why can be found.

Falling Again I find myself
To my right and then to my left.
I cannot catch my pending fall,
Cannot catch anything at all.
The thought races through mind
Of something to stop my fall, if I can find,
A way to stop my pending fate,
To stop it before it is too late.

SOMEBODY

Somebody cares about me.
Always there and happy to be.
Somebody is there that makes me glad,
Keeping me out of trouble and away from bad.

Somebody cares about me.
I am aware but I seem to see,
That somebody is always near
Someone that is loved and dear.

Somebody cares about me.
Looking, reviewing, and seeming to see,
All the things I did right,
Overlooking the errors I might.

Somebody cares about me.
This makes me happy and shout with glee,
Because I know who is, that somebody.
It is the one that loves and lives with me.

FINAL GOODBYE

It is time to say goodbye;
A time to sigh and to cry.
I do not know what to say,
Maybe we will meet another day.
I do not want to leave at this time,
Another day I have to find.

I say goodbye to you with a tear,
With a wonder and with a fear.
What will come or what will be?
I cannot predict or even see.
I turnaround as if to leave,
I made a sign and leave bereaved.

A tear or two runs down my face,
As I pray and leave the lonely place.
I leave without uttering a sound,
With head bent to the ground.
I leave thinking what will be,
Thinking that you I will never to see.

I will never hear you tell a joke,
Remembering the way you used to poke.
I do not look back to take a glance,
Memories in my mind begin to dance.
All that is left is just scenes of the past,
That I hope to be there and always last.

GOOD NIGHT SWEATHEART

I glance upon your face
You lay in bed in your place.
I look as you resting there
Do you really know how much I care?

I wonder if your dreams are sweet
For the one of me no one can beat.
You lay there so peacefully,
I look and wonder what I see.

If you were to leave tonight,
I would lose my will and might.
I have not told you how I feel,
I will have to live with the deal.

I did not say a word as you went to bed;
Words I should have really said.
I watch and wonder what I would do,
If I didn't say the words to you.

I wish I could turn back the clock;
I sit down and take off my socks.
I turn and lay next to you,
I wish I said the words, now I do.

I lay and think what I didn't say;
Thinking maybe I'll say it another day.
What good will my thoughts do,
If I don't say the words to you.
I turn and lightly kiss your face,
I lay next to you in my place.
I whisper gently hoping it will do,
Goodnight Sweetheart, I love you.

HEALTH

Why is everybody rushing around,
As if there are things to be found?
They do not sit upon the porch,
With their feet as hot as a torch.
Watching the sun at evening's eve,
They should stop and breathe.
Time runs faster as we move with it,
Then life hits us with a ton of bricks.
Health is gone and we do not know where,
As we raced just here and there.

Thomas Allen Frith

WOULD SHE?

Sometimes you wonder what to say,
Timing the moment and the day.
There was the one I wish would agree,
And make me happy with all glee.

I did not know what the answer would be,
I just had to ask and wait to see.
It wasn't the most romantic time,
The answer I wanted to find.

Would she live with me and be my wife,
Live from now and all my life?
What would her answer be?
Well I would have to wait to see.

HOW DO I LIVE?

How do I live without the ones I love?
Have peace with the symbol of the dove?

How do I live without you being there,
Your wit and wisdom and flare?

How do I live and care for you?
I just love you, yes I do.

How do I live from day to day?
I just do not know the right thing to say.

How do I live as days goes by?
Sometimes I laugh and some I cry.

How do I live, when things go wrong?
I pray to the one sitting on his throne.

How do I live and show my face,
I visit an old and a new place?

How do I live when life will end?
Remembering what I said and where I have been.

How do I live when you are gone?
I just wondered what I did wrong.

Thomas Allen Frith

How do I live when life is no more?
I open the future by closing life door.

How do I live? I do want to know,
As I travel home to you in the snow.

JUST BEYOND THE MORNING STAR

I know there will be days of sadness and sorrow.
I know that someday there won't be a tomorrow.
For the happiness and time we shared together,
The time we shared for years with each other,
Let me assure you and try to refrain,
That I may ease your concern and pain.
I may not be there with you but I am not far,
I am just beyond the morning star.

As you wake early and fresh each morning,
You get up, stretch and start your yawning,
Look up in the that eastwardly morning sky;
Look at the shining spot with your eyes.
Glance up and take a very long and good look.
Do this before you start to read your book.
I may not be there with you but I am not far,
I am just beyond the morning star.

As you watch and see the bright shining light,
Just remember God's glorious and almighty might.
I sit in his kingdom looking down at you,
Letting you know I still love you, yes I do.
I may not be there waking up this morning,
I will be there to remind you when sunlight's dawning.
I may not be there with you but I am not far,
I am just beyond the morning star.

Look up and throw me a morning kiss,
I will throw one back one you won't miss.
I sit here watching down over you,
I love you. I love you. Yes I do.
I do as I said it many years ago,
Now I am saying because I love you so.
I may not be there with you but I am not far,
I am just beyond the morning star.

I won't go away for I will sit here waiting for you,
As you wake and look up it will be just us two.
As we say our hellos each and every morning,
We will share our love and watch it growing.
It has been there over the long and happy years,
Now I know that this brings on tears.
I may not be there with you but I am not far,
I am just beyond the morning star.

LIFE STYLE

Life goes on as we worry not,
We race on as if time we forgot.
When will we see what we are doing?
Not enjoying it now and ever fooling.
Ourselves to believe we will remain,
And will never walk with a cane.
We do not think of the days ahead,
As we lay our heads down on the bed.
We may reflect upon the things of today,
Sit and think with nothing to say.
We do not try to comprehend,
Not knowing the day it will all end.

We lay our head down at night,
Not worrying about a thing or even any fright.
We assume morning will come as it should do,
For us to rise and have our aches to soothe.
Can one stop and actually think,
Where we are at and at what brink?
It takes life bad deeds to slow us down,
You are talking about a very big frown.
Age become an issue for us,
As we going around and begin to fuss.
We will realize how precious time may be,
If we slow down to watch and see.

LIFE

Do I wonder what life may bring?
A bird singing or a bee string?
Maybe discovery of the mother lobe,
A nice blue bath robe.
What does life have waiting for me?
Maybe riches or maybe that bee.
I try to prepare myself for the best,
Wonder what will bring for the rest.
Life is a game of chance,
Maybe a date or maybe a dance.
It does not foretell it's intents,
What message it tried and was sent.
What do I do if I do not agree?
Run hide or try to flee.
You cannot get away from it,
Until life has gone and been spent.

ANOTHER DAY

I drive along this lonely road,
Be careful, I am always told.
The night time sky spreads about me,
All the stars and the moon I do see.
It is so clear not a cloud in the sky,
A large bright moon I do spy.

The moon beams shine down on me.
I love to see them; they, I do see.
The beams gleam across the water near,
They calm and relieve my desperate fears.
It is as beautiful as the light does reflect,
On the water with the moon, a big yellow speck.

The moon and the stars shine upon me,
It makes me feel good and I want to see.
All the stars and the moon so bright,
All the time and not just in the night.
The peaceful night and morning air,
Leaves the heaven and the blue sky bare.

As the sun breaks across the sky,
One big round red ball I do spy.
A little bright light replaces the night,
As I drive alone and enjoy it in spite.
The sight I do see along the way,
Tell me it is beginning of another day.

God's great sign that he gives to us,
Yet we still want to make a big fuss.
Why do we have to lose the night's dark sky?
As the sun lifts up and grows way up high.
I continue my lonely journey along the way,
As the morning sky brings us another day.

THINKING

I lay here thinking about the day,
Not peeking a sound nor having anything to say.
I wondering what could have been,
As if I could have corrected it there and then.

I lay here thinking about the past,
It seems that time passes very fast.
I review the events of the day,
Thinking of the things that went their way.

I lay here thinking mistakes that were made,
The experience and embarrassment that I paid.
I cannot take back the words I said,
I lie here still in my bed.

I lay here thinking what I should have done,
May be a friend or two I would have won.
If I were to stop to think before I speak,
This is just the first day of the week.

I lay here thinking and trying to sleep,
Not a word do I hear not even a peep.
I am trying to lie here and think,
As my body takes a few winks.

SMILE

I look upon you face so dear,
Is it a sign of pain or fear?
I do not think that is the case,
I watch, you sit, and then pace.

I enjoy seeing what I do see,
Wondering what is up or to be.
I gaze upon your face again.
Any comments I try to refrain.

You communicate to me so differently,
I look back and look to see.
An expression I see on you,
I worry and wonder, that I do.

I begin to ask you why,
Your answer bring tears but I do not cry.
I am proud what you say to me,
I love the expression I see.

My mind races and giving much thought
Wondering what the past has brought.
I watch your face for a long while,
You just say that I make you smile.

NIGHT SLEEP

The night's late is what is said,
Is it time to go to bed?
I am wary and tired
I feel exhausted but all wired.
Can I rest and get some sleep
I pray my Lord to keep?

I feel my body is ready for rest,
A night of sleep at best.
I cannot say I will go to sleep fast,
I think how long will it last.
I lay my head on my bed,
In a way, the next day I dread.

Will God watch over me?
Does he knows; what does he see?
I cannot say I have done him well,
Because my head does not swell.
I have a longing to improve,
I relax and begin to soothe.

I lay wondering what will bring,
As I hear a loud ring.
Groggily I wonder what I hear,
Then I hear the words, I love dear.
Wake up it is time to leave,
I recall and begin to believe.

I fell asleep and did not know,
That all my worries were so bold.
They put me asleep without a care,
Not having a single nightmare.
She pulls the covers and I get cold,
So now up I get and to work I go.

SHE

She planted the flowers in a row,
Not worrying whether someday it will snow.
She works so hard to make them look,
Like the pictures in the book.

She planted a tree on a cold winter day,
Spread around it roots some warm hay.
She hopes the tree will grow big and tall,
Even when she will not be here at all.

She work her fingers till they hurt.
Working with dirt, sod and murk.
She spends long hours in the hot sun,
All of this to her enjoyment and fun.

I watch her as she works on her knees,
A little cough and several little sneezes.
I watch knowing her time may not be long,
It won't be long before she is gone.

The garden that she planted with a lot of care,
Will remind and still be there.
When she is gone away from me,
If in the future I was wise enough to see.

Thomas Allen Frith

I spent too much time to myself,
Keeping busy and working from the shelf.
Working with my limited and lonely time,
As if I had nothing to do or to find.

Now I watch and wonder still,
If there is a magical pill.
I count the days that is speeding by,
Now I am left to sit and cry.

THE PAPER

The morning paper at my door,
A little wet lying on the floor.
It was thrown by a person so dear,
Not a concern or worry or fear.
To get up earlier in order to serve.
To drive down the road and around the curve.
On his way from door to door,
To toss it in the air and let it soar.
In a driveway or in the brush,
As he hurries in a rush.
The morning brings me the news,
Of the people who paid their dues.
A story of the nations at many a tasks,
Maybe a story of criminal past.
A funny cartoon or a little puzzle,
Maybe an ad that gives a nuzzle.
To purchase something I do not need,
To read about someone's plead.
Whatever the reason I do not know,
I want to start to day off slow.

TRIP

Here I sit wondering where I am,
Remembering that I took a tram.
North past many the stores and shops,
Looking out to the mountain tops.
I quietly watch the walking people,
I see behind them a golden steeple.
There across the distant way,
I get a grandeur view of the bay.
Ships slowly inward arriving,
While others steam forward thus departing.
A view of a plane taking off from the port,
Make me wonder more or sorts.
Why is so much bunched so tight?
Wondering about the people on their flight.
Around the curve and the scene is in the past,
Knowing that all sceneries will never last.
Houses and cars are seen rushing by,
There are birds in the sky.
I sit some more and seek to find,
A place to go for a piece of mind.
My minds wonder off in a trance,
Remembering when you took your stance.
The day I left you all alone,
As I boarded my plane and was gone.
I will be returning in just a few days,
I am anxious so much to say.
I missed you much more than you know,
I wish I would never had to go.

Hopefully there will not be another time,
I couldn't even bet that with a dime.
I sit here as the tram comes to the end,
I race to the desk in order to send.
I send a postcard with a special note,
I would be returning by a boat.
Not today nor tomorrow,
My time away from you is all sorrow.
I will be home as soon as I can,
Do not blame me for this tan.
I am wishing you love from afar,
Maybe I will just come home in my car.

Thomas Allen Frith

THESE EYES

These eyes have seen many a thing,
They have seen what love brings.
They have seen the future of tomorrow,
They have seen so much sorrow.

These eyes are tired and very weary,
They have seen the bad and dreary.
Also in their sight has been brought,
Things that they wish were naught.

These eyes have seen good and glory,
Also the results of a false story.
They have seen the joy of the past,
Their eyesight won't forever last.

These eyes may be wet and red,
They tell a story that can be read.
The tears falling from their location,
They cry without other emotion.

These eyes may not see everything,
They shine when they see a ring.
The ring is one that is meant forever,
Given as a present, oh so clever.

These eyes have seen the morning sky,
The sun and moon up so high.
The stars and meteorites speeding by,
The dark colorless nighttime sky.

These eyes have seen many a thing,
What joy and beauty that one may bring.
They see someone special and so dear to me,
For you are the one that I see.

Thomas Allen Frith

THE PAST

Days goes by;
Nights fly too.
Years do not last as long as they did,
The signs of age as one gets old.

Things have changed;
Things are not the same.
Do we want things to remain the way it was?
Do we want memories to be real again?

Love ones are gone;
Love ones mourn.
Life continues on no matter what,
Whether we want it to or not.

Days of past;
Reflect on my mind.
Remembering the fun and the pain of the past,
Remembering what never will return.

Can I change?
Can I cry?
Can someone help me or tell me why?
Why do things gets forgotten as time passes on?

No some things don't;
No some we won't?
All we can do is to think and hope,
Hope for others as time slips on.

TIME

The clock on the wall facing me there,
Sitting high above me in the air.
Ticks the seconds and minutes away,
Telling how much is left of the day.
I watch it working slowly all alone,
There I saw it another minute is gone.
Why does time goes so slow?
The wind travels where does it blow?
I know that time is not always the same,
To watch it is a crying shame.
It goes slow as I look upon,
Afterwards it is rapidly gone.
Tick Tock and a click of time,
It is the speed it travels that is a crime.
When will it be the time that I want?
It never gets there, no it won't.
Hurry, hurry, I loudly cry,
As time slowly passes by.
I give up on watching the time,
I tired of criticizing and giving a whine.
I go back to what I was doing,
Not paying attention as time keeps going.
I look up to my surprise,
Now I am late to my demise.

Thomas Allen Frith

AM I RIGHT OR AM I WRONG?

Am I right or am I wrong?
I do not know but I must be strong.
I decided my fate tonight,
Do I run and take my flight?
Did I choose the right selection?
What if I chose the wrong option?
Am I trying to second guess me?
I want to be right that it must be.
Is it too late to change my mind?
If I chose the right I guess I will find.
Time will tell if I am right or wrong,
By then much time has already gone.
I sit here worrying if I was right,
It only gets me up very uptight.
Time will come to know if I am wrong,
I must sit, wait, and be strong.

AS I GAZE

As I gazed out my back door one day,
I search the trees and the valley small.
I observe the animals and I turn to say,
I think, I love nature as I stand appalled.
Is it real or just another day?

The birds fly so silently by.
The rabbits and raccoons wander around.
I again glance toward the sky,
An eagle or hawk my eyes just found,
Searching for food that may have died.

The green valley grass and green tall trees,
Sends the comfort to me as the scenery I gaze.
Soft and pleasant as a morning can be,
The morning dew shines through the haze.
I see a fox as calm as can be.

What about the deer on the hill?
Is it seeking its little one so deer?
I notice it stops and stands so still,
Turns its head acting with fear.
Then it paces off as if it is not a big deal.

There in the distance I think I spy,
A bear, a wolf or something other.
His movement just caught my eye,
It slowly walks then gently putter.
Raises his head toward the sky.

Maybe he is smelling my scent today,
Maybe he is just grazing the hill.
He looks toward me as if to pay,
A look, a greeting, or maybe a frill.
He races away without a say.

The scene I see each morning at dawn,
Stops me while I begin the day.
I relax to work in the lawn,
A valley and a hill I view in dismay.
Now I see the pretty young fawn.

CAN YOU REMEMBER

Can you remember the night we met?
We both didn't know what we would get.
I saw you look happily my way,
I remember what you had to say.
With a nice smile on your face,
Our eyes joined and locked in place.
You uttered a smile and a nice hello,
I saw a pleasing reaction with a pleasant glow.
I smile back at you and my reply,
Was hello as I caught your lovely eyes.
The person I saw I do not know,
We would join and together grow.
The night went by very nice indeed,
Total honesty I did not heed.
We meet again to my surprise,
That I didn't get to use my disguise.
You weren't prepared for what I had to say,
I was afraid there would not be another day.
A dozen red roses or maybe two,
Was all I knew what to do.
I sent you a dozen divided in half,
Hoping it would lead us on a path.
You took your time to decide what was next,
I know the thought was so complex.
The answer I got a pleasant to hear,
I learned you would say, I love you dear.

Thomas Allen Frith

NOT HERE AT ALL

The wall is full of pictures for everybody to see,
They bring a smile, a joke, even a glee.
Some will say that one looks like so and so,
Isn't he adorable and cute, oh much so?
There is picture of one passed on,
We have missed him since he has been gone.
There is the one of mine,
As least the comments seem to be fine.
There is the baby at different stages,
As she grew up through the ages.
The picture from that one vacation,
There is the one of us on a mission.
The one hiding over there I see,
This is the one I did not like of me.
There are some of who I do not know,
One final look before I have to go.
As I leave the wall before me,
I glance back once as if to see.
Was there one I missed out of view?
Maybe one I wanted to preview.
I leave behind with them in their place,
For now I must leave not a trace.
For you see as I look on the wall,
I was not here, not here at all.

ON THAT LAST AND FINAL DAY

On that last and final day,
Was I able to see and say?
That I loved you and please be brave,
To you my love I gave.

I may not have gave that one last kiss,
Take the others for the one I missed.
We planned for this final day,
It was not meant as a burden to pay.

We knew this day would someday arrive,
We put it from our minds and try to survive.
Would it be simple or more complex,
Not knowing who be first or who will be next?

We lost other love ones as years went past,
Some we hate to say it, someone is last.
Our time is limited on this earth,
This was determined before our birth.

We cannot buy another single day,
No matter how we live or what we say.
Today was the day that was determined for me,
I hope you accept it and know it was to be.

What time we spent together on this earth,
It is now my time for the new birth.
Will I meet the ones that went before me?
I don't know but you I hope to see.

When we meet again in the life hereafter,
I will be waiting sitting on a special rafter.
With a special smile and gleam in my eye,
That love one joining me I will spy.

Until that day that is set for you,
I will Love God and make do.
Till we meet again and sing to God,
Together for eternity praising with a special nod,

We were meant to be together before this day,
Together again is what God does say.
I loved you more than I ever let you know,
So darling be happy as to heaven I go.

MEMORIES

I try to recall my young childhood,
Things that may be misunderstood.
I remember building that old tree house,
Chasing a fast avoiding field mouse.
There is the time I found that fish,
Carried it home and put in a dish.
Never forgetting the time with the pump,
Ripped my finger open, made my heart thump.
There is the time I stepped on a nail,
My brother threw clods at me without fail.
The one time a picnic we had,
With my brothers, mom and even dad.
The hard work to bring in the crop,
The work we did with the mop.
There is the times playing in the mud,
The time I fell with such a thud.
Riding in the chair down the side of a cliff,
Acting as if it was actually a lift.
A time swimming in the nude,
Riding the river in an inner tube.
The swimming lessons given by dad,
I learned to swim really not bad.
How about the time seeking a fish?
How about the time tangled in the mesh?
The one time I was crushed oh so light,
I was sore for many a night.
There is the time I was digging for gold,
There would be none I was told.

Thomas Allen Frith

Some things I would try to forget,
The first time puffing on a cigarette.
The time I was being manly and bold,
Without a coat I dashed into the cold.
There are many events that I do not recall,
Not in my memory, not at all

PEOPLE

Red hair, black hair, white and brown,
There are so many different people around.
Do they really measure up to me?
I guess they may but we will have to see.
Some seem strange, some kind and some weird,
Clean shaven, hairy and some with beards.

Why am I here I question myself?
Everybody is talking but am I deaf?
For it seems their talking was for me,
With me being here was not to be.
People seems so bold and cold
They do whatever they learned or told.

Thomas Allen Frith

THE KISS

I gently press my lips for a kiss.
Do I close my eyes and wonder what I will miss?
If I keep them open wide to see,
What will I see but someone looking at me?

I press my lips against you so sweet,
My mind begins to churn as our lips meet.
What is this feeling that I begin to feel?
Am I dreaming or is it real?

I have feelings that I love you so,
Why should I stop but let it go.
We kiss with all our might,
If someone was watching, oh what a sigh.

We need to break and come up for air.
Gradually my hands runs through your hair.
Oh this is too much to stop it here,
I want you to need me and have me near.

Our lips are locked in a tight embrace,
Our hearts beat at a rapid pace.
We break our lips to grasp for air,
Is it love or do we care?

THE MAN

I see a man across the way,
I smile and wave as if to say,
Hello stranger whoever you might be,
You are not from here this I see.

What is your reason for traveling by here?
You seem to be roaming and going nowhere.
He politely waves back and gives a smile.
I have been here before but it has been a while.

I ask his name as if to know,
He tells me and I remember him so.
He was a friend that left back sometime.
He left behind friends and success he did climb.

He is a nice older man that is rich I find,
World experience, Polite, and very kind.
For you see the man that was to be,
Was not a stranger but was only me.

Thomas Allen Frith

THE STRUGGLE

I looked at the wall and noticed a clock.
I watch its second hand and hear its tock.
What time is it as I try to seek?
I look; glare at it; and take a peek.
Oh, it cannot be that time as I think.
Because, I am late to take a drink.
The drink I need because you see.
I have to take a pill to help what ails me.
I look again to be sure.
I need to seek my aiding cure.
Oh it is not as late as I thought.
As I struggle with myself and fought.
I must get up and take my pill.
If I really want to get well.

TIME PASSES

Sometimes time passes all so slow,
Then at others you wonder where it goes.
It is said that time stands still;
Passes along at its own will.
People say at times time flies by.
Is this what we want if we are not ready to die?
Some wants to put time on hold;
We cannot do that I am told.
Time ticks on so gently by.
Why so slow? I wonder why.
We do not want time to use us;
We complain and throw a fuss.
Is time really on our side?
Is it like the ocean tides?
Going back and forth to and fro.
Oh, why don't we just let time go?

Thomas Allen Frith

TRAIN

I hear a train coming down the track.
Is it a dream or is it a fact?
The whistle blows once then twice,
A sound I love and think it is nice.
I wait to see the cars do pass,
I know it can be a major task.
One car, two car I do count,
How many more? Do I doubt?
Another one, then another it is to be,
I wonder if the caboose I will be able to see.
I wait seeking that little red caboose,
My sight I stay and not turn loose.
I keep a watchful eye for the end,
Trying to see the car around the bend.
Is it here? Can you see it now?
I wonder where and then a wow.
The little red caboose dotted the air,
Around the bend and there in great flare.
I see it. I see it. I shout out loud,
As if it dropped out of the clouds.
Coming closer to my dear delight,
I guess I could ride it if I might.
It passes me by with a rattle of the track,
Telling me tomorrow it will be back.
I watch it disappear out of sight,
It leaves me remembering its great might.

WHAT IF YOU WERE TO LEAVE ME BEHIND

What if you were to leave me behind?
I would search for you but never find,
The love we shared and still have strong.
I will weep and cry. Is that wrong?
The days and nights will not be the same.
I am like an animal that is wounded and lame.
I have already missed you I guess you know.
I know I have no choice I have to let you go.
When life ends so unexpectedly,
It is hard to handle so hear my plea.
While you are here and still with me,
I want your love and not your sympathy.

What if you were to leave me behind?
My adoring love will remember you as kind.
Life is short but our lives were long.
I don't want you to go, is that wrong?
I know I must let you go.
Honey I will miss you so.
May I ask you just one more thing?
Remember me as you meet the King.
That may be pure selfishness on my part.
I love you and cannot get you out of my heart.
One last thing before my final goodbye,
I love you and now I must go and cry.

Thomas Allen Frith

WHAT IS TECHNOLOGY?

What is technology? That is hard to say
What it is was not what it was yesterday.
Is it a way to make things better?
A way to make us madder?

Is it something that helps us work?
Is it a plaything just by a quirk?
I cannot define technology today,
Some will disagree not matter what I say.

I do know that there is a priority,
To install and use what is called technology.
One will disagree what I have to say,
It will ruin society as we know today.

What may seem like a benefit to us,
It will dictate and make its use a must.
It will be the downfall of society,
Destroy all forms of civil morality.

What may seem like a great benefit,
I wish it never started or at least it would quit.
Being an issue and everyone's plea.
What is? What really is technology?

WITHOUT LOVE

Without love what would I have done?
Without love would I have had all the fun?
Without love would you have put up with me?
Without love would we be happy as can be?

Without love what future would we have had?
Without love our lives would have been bad.
Without love I could not say I love you.
Without love I would have been just blue.

Without love how would you really feel about me?
Without love I am glad that I did not have to see.
Without love I would not have my best friend.
Without love I would not have been pinned

Without love how could you overlook my faults?
Without love our memories would not be in the vault.
Without love what else can I really say?
Without love you would not be here today.

Thomas Allen Frith

REFLECTIONS

Reflections of shadows display,
I look and see this very day.
Reflections of mountain so high,
On the waters of the lake, Oh my!
Reflections on a mirror a face display,
Of a person rising for the day.
Reflections of my childhood's older years,
Things I remember and to me hold dear.
All the reflections our mind does see,
Images of the real but real may not be.
Reflections of things I live with today,
In life I lived and with age I pay.